MAKE AMERICA THINK AGAIN:

A ROADMAP TO COMMON SENSE FOR THE MODERN AMERICAN

E. JOI COX

Copyright © 2025 E. Joi Cox
All rights reserved.
ISBN: 9798306921174

*TO THOSE WHO USE THE MIND
PRUDENTLY TO BETTER HUMANITY.*

TABLE OF CONTENTS

- **INTRODUCTION** 7
  - How To Use This Book 10
  - Purpose 10
  - Suggested Materials 10
- **RESISTANCE** 11
  - How to Explore Resistance 14
  - Good vs. Bad Reasoning 15
  - **Chapter 1 Assignments** 17
- **HABITS** 19
  - Bad Habits 22
  - Poor Reasoning 23
  - The Good News 24
  - A Note On Curiosity 25
  - Prompts to Amplify Your Curiosity 26
  - **Chapter 2 Assignments** 27
- **ABILITIES** 29
  - The Power of Words 33
  - Confirmation Bias 35
  - **Chapter 3 Assignments** 36
- **AVAILABILITIES** 37
  - Challenges to Availability 40
  - Hold Space For Resistance 42
  - Make Time For (Good) Habits 44
  - Encourage the Energy for Abilities 45
  - **Chapter 4 Assignments** 49
- Conclusion 51
- Author Biography 54
- Works Cited 55

INTRODUCTION

Common sense is becoming harder and harder to find these days. In the United States, basic reasoning skills have become so diminished that nearly all aspects of life are affected - social, professional, romantic, medical - in increasingly dangerous ways.

Disagreements and misunderstandings lead to highway shootings[1], customer service employees and white collar executives alike behave inappropriately while on the clock[2], dishonesty has several common terms for people in the dating scene (ghosting, breadcrumbing[3], roaching[4]), and preventable chronic diseases are the leading cause of deaths in the United States[5].

Common sense tells me that road rage-induced arguments among strangers should not lead to murder. Common sense tells me that things like stealing from an employer, drinking while on the clock, or harassing employees is wrong. Common sense tells me that *honesty is the best policy* when it comes to relationships of all kinds. And finally, common sense tells me that it is my responsibility to take care of my most basic needs if I want to live a fulfilling life.

But common sense - **sound and prudent judgment based on a simple perception of the situation or facts[6]; an informal standard of behaviors and ethics that are accepted by a group, society, or culture** - is not so common anymore. While a growing number of people agree that *ghosting* is an acceptable way to leave a job or romantic relationship, for example, the *commonality* of prudent judgment diminishes. As a result, our quality of life is severely affected, families are divided, and countless individuals feel isolated and emotionally strained. The 2024 national elections alone point to deepening divisions as over 90 million eligible voters did not participate in the already contentious contest.

I care about common sense because I care about critical thinking - the objective analysis and evaluation of an issue in order to form a judgment. As a philosopher who has spent a number of years teaching key principles of critical thinking and ethics to adults and youths, I have seen firsthand the positive role that objective analysis plays in creating a rational society.

But Americans as a whole are not ready to think critically.

We fail to perceive serious issues objectively, causing undesirable patterns to appear (increased shootings in schools, on highways, and in other public spaces), **good ideas to get overlooked** (in science, business, politics, and the arts alike)[7], **and preventable dilemmas to worsen** (the obesity epidemic[8] and health care crisis quickly come to mind[9]). Instead of funding organizations to sufficiently research <u>and</u> tackle these issues, too many Americans *resist* a standard of behaviors that might resolve the issues. By insisting that the government cannot be trusted to do what's needed[10], or, simply *not* admitting that people like benefiting from some of these problems[11], Americans continue to drive the country towards danger.

Rather than present yet another critical thinking textbook, <u>I offer an exploration of what is preventing Americans from seeing that</u>, whether we like it or not, <u>we're all in this together</u>.

Common sense is the most basic road we use to 'travel' safely as a society. Over time as that road has filled with potholes, signs faded, and signals became non-operational, roadblocks appeared, prompting individuals to take detours away from a serviceable and worthwhile path.

Make America Think Again begins at the roadblock to finding basic common ground - **resistance** to unfamiliar ideas/activities.

It moves on to explore the familiar routes that brought us to this impasse - the **habits** and **abilities** that make up our daily life.

And it ends with a fresh look at the road ahead of us - **availabilities**.

This approach gets the average American <u>ready</u> to think critically. It is a concise invitation for Americans to consider, recognize, and implement detours away from the shortsightedness, reactivity, and defensiveness fueling various interpersonal AND national issues.

~~~

I am a pole fitness coach, yoga teacher, and personal trainer. I regularly teach in environments that are "safe" spaces. These spaces cultivate, promote, and foster *discomfort, frustration, trial and error, repeated failure,* and *actual injury.* In those same spaces, we cultivate, promote, and encourage small wins, experimentation, reflection, personal bests, and milestones.

No matter the discipline or apparatus, NO ONE starts their journey in a comfortable state. We discuss injuries, limitations, challenges, fears, and anything else that might stand in the way of learning a new skill. Without addressing these initial *barriers,* progress and learning simply cannot take place. In other words, students cannot proceed on the path to acquiring new skills .

In the same way that a coach guides budding athletes towards success, Make America Think Again is a roadmap to the door of modern problems. By using smoother and more sustainable intellectual paths, **conversations become easier and more productive, confusion is reduced, solutions to problems appear more readily, and various other life-improving outcomes are experienced (including being more comfortable with your own mind).**

In the end, when it comes time to face big challenges and uncomfortable situations, you will feel more prepared.

HOW TO USE THIS BOOK

M.A.T.A. is a self-paced, four-chapter exploration of common sense for the modern American. It is recommended that you take about one week to complete each chapter. Some terminology may be familiar from academic courses or conversations you've seen on socials. As a result, there is PLENTY of supplementary information online if you'd like more examples or definitions.

This is not, however, a formal college course. It is a gentle introduction to thinking well and a road map for developing common sense. **Understanding the concepts covered and completing the activities provided will make conversations easier and more productive, reduce confusion, uncover options for problem-solving, and produce various other life-improving outcomes.**

PURPOSE

Common sense is not so common anymore. The standard for sensible and prudent behaviors has diminished, leaving families broken, communities divided, and many people feeling isolated and emotionally strained. As the nation divests from solution-driven programs while seeing increases in preventable dangers and deaths, it is time for Americans to think (again). ***Make America Think Again* is a concise invitation for Americans to think more clearly by exploring detours away from shortsightedness, reactivity, and defensiveness.**

This book takes readers on a journey to explore how their own *resistance*, *habits*, *abilities*, and *availabilities* contribute to thinking well. Each person's application of these topics may differ, and assignments will provide opportunities to re-develop one's cognitive roadmap. In the end, readers will be better prepared to face challenges, consider big questions, face uncomfortable situations, and handle difficult emotions.

SUGGESTED MATERIALS

A Journal - Hand-written, electronic, in a dedicated app, on a white board, or via social media. However you do it, this is how you will keep track of your activities & reflections.

An Open Mind - Remain open to how, when, and why ideas apply to your life.

Chapter 1

<u>RESISTANCE</u>

THE REFUSAL TO ACCEPT OR COMPLY WITH SOMETHING; THE ABILITY TO NOT BE AFFECTED BY SOMETHING

Resistance is a powerful and effective block on the road to new experiences. But if you are reading this book voluntarily, you have already agreed to take your thinking down a new path. Kudos to you, even though you might not know exactly where it's going to lead.

This isn't going to be sunshine and unicorns. Simply *thinking* about difference can put us in a bad mood and, seemingly instinctively, our internal chatter chimes in to protect us from being turned into a 'snowflake', and protect our free will from being taken away.

STOP LISTENING!
THERE IS NO TIME FOR THIS
AM I BEING ATTACKED? I AM BEING ATTACKED!

Refusing to accept a thing and *actively* avoiding being affected by it, forces us to stick to familiar patterns. This can look like only socializing with specific people for years, exclusively consuming the same flavors and brands every day, and refusing to drive unknown routes to/from work...in short, we exist within comfortable boundaries without questioning (or even being aware) that other destinations exist.

> Sometimes resistance comes from feeling mentally ill-equipped to handle new ideas - we literally don't know what or how to think, and that is scary.

> Sometimes resistance comes from not knowing how to add to a conversation - because looking and sounding unintelligent in public damages our self-image.

> Sometimes resistance road blocks come from legitimate concerns - one food-poisoning incident prevented me from eating eggplant for nearly 20 years.

The appearance of these road blocks can make us default to emotions that have worked in the past such as anger, sarcasm, or panic. Which is unfortunate, because these emotions don't end up addressing new ideas, improving our image, or accurately identifying potential dangers.

These emotions can prevent us from seeing reality.

Common sense - sound and prudent judgment based on a simple perception of the situation or facts - **invites us to slow down, and take a look at what is actually happening.**

HOW TO EXPLORE RESISTANCE

Is my guard up?

What am I resisting right now?

Have I become defensive in this moment?

I've never heard that word before, what does it mean?

I saw a reel online where someone was talking about that idea, but I didn't watch it.

That made me sick once. Why do you like it so much?

I don't agree with what you're saying.

No, I don't understand but I'm happy to listen to you explain a little more....

~~~

As you encounter a new and unfamiliar idea, person, place, or thing, be honest about that fact:

THIS IS NEW AND UNFAMILIAR

AND,

pause right there.

THEN,
notice if the urge to resist the interaction entirely arises,
take a breath,
and consider which of the phrases above might apply to the situation.

GOOD VS. BAD REASONING

Noticing that a road block has (suddenly) appeared is the first step to taking a detour. You get to perceive the facts of the situation, and decide what happens next. This book isn't about me telling you what to think or do, but now is a good time to discuss how we reach conclusions aka *reasoning*.

In my lifetime, negativity has been more popular on the news, in movies, and politically than inspiring and constructive topics - *if it bleeds, it leads*. Blood, violence, and anger evoke passionate parts of our minds, and it's natural to have strong opinions and vivid experiences attached to these topics. However, if fight, flight, or ignorance are also attached to those opinions and experiences, then reasoning may be biased.

BAD reasoning is the kind of thinking that leads to an unhelpful, contrary, irrational, unacceptable, unjustified, or unwarranted conclusion, given the available information. Bad reasoning is also frequently tied to the kinds of passionate thinking listed above.

Consider a road rage argument that escalates to one driver firing his gun at the other man's car, killing a child passenger.

This is an example of bad reasoning because firing the gun was neither helpful nor warranted given the available information. The death of the child was unjustified, and it is unacceptable to think that all arguments should proceed in this manner (because it would lead to much higher mortality rates).

"Having a loaded gun readily available in a tense situation is a road to disaster[12]*."*

The offender in this example had a choice between firing and not firing his weapon at something that was no longer a threat. He likely did not even know if other passengers were in the vehicle when he *reasoned* to a conclusion that was contrary to the survival of everyone involved.

GOOD reasoning is characterized by conclusions that are well-supported. We use reliable sources, personal experiences, and connected ideas to decide what should be done or believed. To maximize safety, *common* sense requires good reasoning.

Basing our actions on *bad* or *irrational* reasoning can be lethal, but it can also set us up for confusion and isolation. Inconsistencies start to appear (*I am justified in doing this, but no-one else is*), we may ostracize entire groups of people (*Only certain types of men should own guns*), and ultimately, we may limit our experiences (*It's not safe to travel to that city*). Worst of all, **the longer we hold on to bad reasoning, the harder it is to think or act differently.**

Every day we have choices to make. Some of those choices seem simple and insignificant, while others are difficult and meaningful. Especially for the difficult and meaningful ones, feelings of resistance can creep up insisting that we make the easiest possible choice. Unfortunately, reality tells us that the easy route is not always the best, the healthiest, or safest road to take.

Common sense asks that we use reality to *inform* our decision-making. **In order to Make America Think Again good reasoning must be popularized.** We must see that common sense - reasoning in a way that provides good, COMMON outcomes - makes life better.

AND if the idea of reasoning well is giving you a bad feeling or making you tense up right now, use the assignments on the next page to explore why.

CHAPTER 1 ASSIGNMENTS

WATCH/LISTEN TO AN EPISODE OF "THE PEOPLE I KNOW"

Season 1: The White Guys I Know

www.joiofdance.org/thepeopleiknow

The People I Know is a podcast I created to casually discuss philosophical concepts with the diverse people I have met throughout my life. Use the link provided, pick an episode from the first season (or binge them all), and reflect on relevant concepts from this week's lesson.

FIND EXAMPLES OF REASONING IN SOCIAL MEDIA

Set a timer for 5 minutes and see how many examples of GOOD and BAD reasoning you can find online or in your social media feed.

1 - What reasoning was well-supported? What reliable sources were mentioned?

2 - What conclusions were unjustified or irrational? Was anything contrary to what you believe?

REFLECTION

Take 5-15 minutes to journal by hand, phone, audio or video.

1 - What kinds of ideas induce your resistance? What type of response is typical for you?

2- How would you rate YOUR ability to reason? How would you rate the ability to reason of your friends/family? Why?

Chapter 2

<u>HABITS</u>

A SETTLED OR REGULAR TENDENCY OR PRACTICE, ESPECIALLY ONE THAT IS HARD TO GIVE UP

Take 2 minutes to list TEN activities that you do regularly. Feel free to write them down, put them in your phone, or record a video.

What activities do you do

Hourly   Bi-weekly   Annually

Daily   Monthly   Semi-Annually

Weekly   Seasonally   By Decade

Autopilot - a device for keeping an aircraft on a set course without the intervention of the pilot - is a great example for understanding regularity in our lives. During safe portions of flight, pilots use the autopilot feature to regulate important variables that keep the plane flying. A too-often underrated aspect of this device, is the underlying equations, parameters, factors, and variables that have been tested and re-tested to ensure the feature works. If even one of these essential underlying variables is flawed in any way, autopilot will not function.

Similarly, countless daily habits set our course through life. From brushing our teeth to drinking morning coffee, to walking the dog or picking the kids up from school, certain parameters and specific factors regulate our lives.

Think again on the activities you do on a regular basis, like brushing your teeth. Now imagine if, twice daily, you had to figure out **how** to identify and then hold a toothbrush. If you had to distinguish toothpaste from lotion or other substances in your bathroom, How long would it take to research the best brushing method. This important habit would be stressful! Literal additional energy for our minds and bodies to exert when they could be acting automatically.

The culmination of daily habits (plus a few other unique details) shapes the route YOU take through life and explains why YOUR route looks different from that of the next person. Brushing with your right hand defines how your bathroom counter is organized. Drinking coffee or tea everyday affects your monthly budget. Walking the pet or dropping kids off for activities shifts your schedule for the rest of the week.

Habits simplify life, but when poor habits start to define and shape our route, the road may become bumpy - stressful, confusing, and inefficient.

BAD HABITS
THEORETICAL VS. REAL-WORLD CONSEQUENCES

In theory, working more than 8 hours a day is good because my paycheck will be bigger. But in reality I will be exhausted, have less time to spend with my friends/family, and my workplace will expect this unhealthy behavior from me.

In theory, getting dinner from the nearest drive-thru is ok because it's convenient and inexpensive. But in reality I'll order unhealthy food (fried and lacking adequate nutrition), end up eating in my car, and spend more money than if I had cooked my own meal.

In theory, checking social media notifications immediately on my phone is a way to make sure I stay in touch with friends. But in reality I spend more time on my phone, get distracted once I am in an app, and lose track of time due to the way social media are designed.

On paper, there's no harm in working long hours, eating at a fast food chain, or using social media. Unfortunately, once our context changes - once we look at reality[13], research findings[14], and our own experiences[15] - we can see real-world consequences to these habits.

To be clear, these activities aren't necessarily *bad*. Writing this book has required MANY long hours and a certain fast food chain will always be my go-to for fries. However, **when we know that we don't want the consequence of an activity, and we repeatedly do that activity anyway, it can be considered a bad habit**. And when bad habits combine to construct the paths we take daily, poor reasoning replaces or prevents common sense.

POOR REASONING

Examples of poor reasoning include making hasty generalizations (*everyone from that state is ignorant*), holding false beliefs (*the sun revolves around the earth*), and ineffective actions (*having less employees during a busy shift*). Using poor reasoning, we run the risk of being wrong, ignoring and insulting entire groups of people, and sounding unintelligent.

Rhetoric is another common method of poor reasoning which quickly grabs the attention of an audience. Some rhetorical devices seem innocent enough (like a political candidate using *alliteration* to make their slogan memorable), while other devices use clever or hidden psychological methods (like a commercial showing images of a heartwarming reunion between old friends to sell their product - *pathos*).

Poor reasoning dissuades us from looking at facts, considering consequences and additional possibilities.

Poor reasoning makes it harder to know what is true, understand that information is missing, and distinguish facts from falsehoods.

Identifying good and bad reasoning, learning how to dissect falsehoods, and deciding when to be persuaded by rhetoric takes practice. But once we see that these examples of wear and tear have impacted our path, we can start to reconstruct it.

Reflect on the habits you listed at the beginning of the chapter:

Which of your habits is something that has 'always' been done in your family?
Is there a more modern or efficient way to do it?

Which of your habits is something you learned to do as a child?
How do you know that you're doing it correctly?

How many habits are automated (using auto-pay or other technology)?
Is there a risk of data or security breaches?

Is your autopilot system working as accurately as it could be? Is it time for any of the important functions to be recalibrated? Are there any variables that are secretly sabotaging your goals or quality of life?

THE GOOD NEWS

The good news is that M.A.T.A. isn't about you being "smart" or "stupid" - it's about being open to making relevant improvements. Remember how the first chapter invited us to *acknowledge resistance*? The next step is to simply *take a good look at what we've been doing.*

If poor reasoning has influenced bad habits in your life, the good news is that it is possible to use better reasoning moving forward. Simply examining habits paves the way to review, modify, and reconfigure our life as needed, making our journey more effortless.

A NOTE ON CURIOSITY

Don't believe everything you hear...but remain curious about what's being said.

We're all bound to experience periods of life where we enjoy bad habits such as a poor diet, reckless driving, or being deceitful. Over time, common sense makes clear that these habits negatively impact our quality of life. At some point we are faced with a choice - adapt or risk disease, being lonely, and dying young.

One habit, however, tends to get brushed aside the older we get - curiosity. As one of the brightest lights on our path, **curiosity encourages us to seek out information** (*Is that a caution signal ahead?*), **appreciate details** (*It is a caution signal, but not for my lane of traffic*), **and connect ideas** (*I still need to be aware because people will begin merging into my lane soon*).

There are additional cognitive habits that improve our quality of life[16], and you should certainly research them if your *curiosity* has been piqued. But I'll end this chapter with a simple list of curiosity prompts to incorporate into your daily, weekly, or monthly routines.

In time, you might find that the more curiosity habits you embrace, the less you need habits that negatively impact your quality of life such as apathy, disinterest, indifference, or absent-mindedly going with the flow.

PROMPTS TO AMPLIFY YOUR CURIOSITY

<u>**Wonder why**</u> something is made a certain way.
- How did someone make this thing? Why did they have this idea?
- What doesn't work about this thing or idea?
- What was the environment like when this thing/idea came to be? (Social, political, etc.)
- Who is affected by this thing/idea being this way? Who is not affected?
- Could this be done another way?

<u>**Question how**</u> someone reached a conclusion.
- What evidence did this person have? What evidence did they not have?
- If I had the same information, would I have reached the same conclusion?
- Did this person reach this conclusion impartially?
- What emotions might have affected how someone got to this conclusion?

<u>**Ask where else & when**</u> a statement is true.
- Is this also true in another State or Country? For another generation (past or future)?
- Is a statement true for me, my spouse/neighbor/friends? Why/why not?
- Is this true in the morning and at night? In a different season?

<u>**Understand what**</u> is being said.
- Repeat what you have heard
- Rephrase what someone says in a conversation. Ask if you heard them correctly.
- Identify facts from fiction, objectivity from metaphor or jargon.
- Identify unfamiliar words/phrases/concepts (and then define them).

**Remember, becoming curious MENTALLY does not mean you have to reach conclusions yourself or ACT any differently.

CHAPTER 2 ASSIGNMENTS

WATCH/LISTEN TO AN EPISODE OF "THE PEOPLE I KNOW"
Season 2: The Mixed Chicks I Know
www.joiofdance.org/thepeopleiknow
Use the link provided, pick an episode from the second season (or binge them all), and reflect on relevant concepts from this week's lesson.

FIND EXAMPLES OF HABITS IN SOCIAL MEDIA
Set a timer for 5 minutes and see how many examples of HABITS you can find online or in your social media feed.

How frequently is the habit done? Is the habit good/bad? Is it healthy/harmful?

REFLECTION
Take 5-15 minutes to journal by hand, phone, audio or video.

1 - It's often said that mistakes and pain are necessary for growth. How true do you think this is when it comes to developing good habits? How does making mistakes encourage or deter you from improving your habits?

2 - What happens to people who are not curious? Consider the children in your life (if applicable). How does youthful curiosity differ from curiosity in adults?

Chapter 3

ABILITIES

POSSESSION OF THE MEANS OR SKILL TO DO SOMETHING; TALENT, SKILL, OR PROFICIENCY IN A PARTICULAR AREA

Let's start this chapter with an egoistic reflection
...and note the difference between *egoism* and *egotism*.

Take 3 minutes to think about your abilities

What <u>CAN</u> you do?

What is your physical fitness level? What activities best demonstrate your flexibility and strength?

When on a team or group project, which role do you play (organizer, idea-generator, motivator, researcher, leader, etc.)?

How would you measure your status/success academically? Professionally? Socially?

To who/what are you most dependable?

What word(s) best describes your command of your first language? What additional languages do you speak/understand?

How would you measure your level of compassion?

How well do you think you can differentiate between your own ideas/feelings and those of other people?

How often do you engage in levity? Do you know any good jokes off the top of your head?

Common sense is about using the abilities of our mind reasonably. Actions such as denying reality, using words incorrectly, lying, resisting growth, and ignoring new information exemplify unreasonable thinking.

Unfortunately, negativity is so popular that talking about *inabilities* and *negations* is customary. Nowadays for many, negative talk (especially self-talk) is natural even though it can be damaging to our health[17] and actually contradicts how to improve behaviors.

Years ago during a professional development training, I learned the simple yet invaluable effect of <u>*positive*</u> reminders. Instead of thinking *"don't forget to call dad later"*, for example, it is more helpful to think *"remember to call dad later"*. Such a subtle difference, but it *hits different* because **positivity is not the same as punishment or shaming <u>and</u> we are reinforcing the behavior we actually want.**

Similarly, we are less stressed talking about the things we CAN do than we are talking about those things we CANNOT do. Talking about things we CANNOT do can invoke negative memories, toxic relationships, and unpleasant emotions. On the contrary, by talking about things that we ARE capable of and the talents we DO HAVE, we invite positive memories and encouraging emotions such as pride, appreciation, and confidence.

Look back at the reflection.
Did you use positive or negative language to describe your abilities?

The reflection questions at the start of this chapter direct us to think about *objective reality* aka FACTS. Complaining and negative talk feels good from time to time, but it neither represents nor improves reality - it makes it worse.

This road on which we are traveling has potholes and barriers. We can drive around them (complain) and take alternate routes (talk negatively), but the problems are still there. If we are serious about keeping the road operational, at some point we have to look at and measure each pothole and look into what each barrier blocks.

As you shift your focus to recognize abilities and their details, remain open to understanding how you have been navigating *around* reality by ruminating on negativities that do not describe what's really there.

This chapter is about compelling our minds to function in an objective, impersonal, and unbiased way. Improving our common sense isn't just about staying positive, it's about <u>assessing reality</u> enough for a common understanding or judgment to be reached.

The rest of this chapter will inspect more of what we are able to do and reveal possibilities we've not yet considered.

THE POWER OF WORDS
"Raise your words, not your voice. It is rain that grows flowers, not thunder."
-*Rumi*

One of my favorite things about being human is our ability to use words. We use them to communicate thoughts and emotions, to give information, and warn of danger. As new words are created for inventions and innovations, we "continuously encounter new ways of describing the world around us"[18].

Other methods of communication also shape our lives - such as non-verbal communication with children and pets, and body language that helps or hurts a job interview. But we are now going to focus on a critical point:

The words we use create our reality.

I usually introduce myself as *"Joi, with an i"* so people 1- understand how to pronounce my name since it's not spelled traditionally, and 2- remember that there is something special about me. It tends to stick in their memory better than if I simply say my name, and occasionally it leads to deeper conversation. Instead of hoping that someone notices the unique spelling, or spending time correcting people, I use my words to create the reality I want to experience.

Let's return to our roadmap with a real-world example that also highlights the serious role words play in our daily lives. In 2024 the Federal Highway Administration set new rules about funny electronic freeway signs, expressing that "signs should be clear, simple, command attention and respect, and provide time for response"[19]. Signs that use humor or pop culture references can confuse and distract drivers. As someone who enjoys these punny signs during my commute (such as the OG *Click It or Ticket*), I admit that my eyes have indeed lingered on one or more of these confusing signs instead of remaining alert to road hazards.

33

The words we choose describe our reality as well as our future.

Quite literally, highway signs are designed to alert us to something that is farther down the road we are on - our future - and signal us to prepare for what is ahead. If the sign is confusing, expired, or contains errors, we are likely to ignore the message even if a hazard still lies ahead. In short, we see words, we form a belief about those words, and we act on that belief.

What reality do the words about your own abilities describe? For me, the statement "I am an active person" not only reflects my past behaviors (teaching, training, and dancing 5+ days a week), it also leads me to believe that my future actions should fit into that description. Conversely, if I respond "I am not an active person," I will start believing that I do not need to participate in physical activities on a regular basis because that's not what non-active people do.

I cannot tell you what to believe about yourself or others. Developing common sense, though, relies on the correct use of words and accurate descriptions of reality to reach practical conclusions. A road filled with errors and inaccuracies leads to impractical conclusions. And persistent, unexamined use of that road leads to hazards.

~~~

Do you remember discussing autopilot in Chapter 2?
Habits come from our mind implementing a set of beliefs.

CONFIRMATION BIAS

Confirmation bias - **the tendency to interpret new evidence as confirmation of one's existing beliefs or theories** - is a phenomenon that pilots, especially, work hard to be aware of. Instead of seeking information that gives a full picture of the weather ahead, for example, a pilot might only seek information that supports their belief that 'the weather doesn't look that bad', potentially leading to a flight plan that takes them directly into danger. In aviation, this type of reasoning has contributed to numerous incidents and tragedies, but how does it apply to the average person?

Confirmation bias can affect *how* we gather the information we need. Statements from people, websites, or social media pages we simply don't like may get ignored, and "we tend not to ask a question if we think we might not like the answer[20]". Not only does this amount to gathering less information that is relevant, the quality of our questioning (and the consequently the quality of our behaviors) suffers.

The questions at the beginning of the chapter assess your current state, <u>not</u> determine your future. Unfortunately, some who don't like the answers to those questions will get trapped in a self-defeating habit loop:

I'm not an active person, so I won't be an active person.
I never learned to speak any other languages, so I'm not going to learn any other languages.
I'm not a funny person, so I don't need to learn any jokes.

Common sense guides us to <u>use</u> our ability of reasoning. As we carefully strengthen the connection between our thoughts and actions, we also learn to *enhance and expand* any other abilities we want.

CHAPTER 3 ASSIGNMENTS

WATCH/LISTEN TO AN EPISODE OF "THE PEOPLE I KNOW"
Season 3: The Black Folks I Know
www.joiofdance.org/thepeopleiknow

Use the link provided, pick an episode from the third season (or binge them all), and reflect on relevant concepts from this week's lesson.

FIND EXAMPLES OF ABILITIES IN SOCIAL MEDIA
Set a timer for 5 minutes and see how many examples of ABILITIES you can find online or in your social media feed.

1 - How do you know about someone's fitness level or ability to tell jokes? How can you measure someone's responsibility? What evidence is presented?

2 - What are the measures of success that you see online? How do you know whether someone is UNsuccessful?

REFLECTION
Take 5-15 minutes to journal by hand, phone, audio or video.

1 - What words do you use most often to describe the following topics:
- Your friends
- Your family
- Your romantic life
- Your hobby
- Your job
- Your future

2 - Using a thesaurus, find 2-5 new words to describe each topic.

3 - Write a brief reflection on how the new words do or do not change your perceptions of the topics.

Chapter 4

AVAILABILITIES

THE QUALITY OF BEING ABLE TO BE USED OR OBTAINED; THE STATE OF BEING OTHERWISE UNOCCUPIED; FREEDOM TO DO SOMETHING

Consider *things you <u>want</u>*.
Not the things you ***should*** want or need, or that others tell you to want.

Listen only to yourself for 7 minutes and make a list:

What do you <u>WANT</u> to do?

-In one month

                              -In three months

                                                        -In six months

-One year from now

                              -Five years from now

                                                        -In twenty years

-After work/school today

                              -When you wake up

                                                        -When you are alone

-When you are with family

                              -When you are with friends

L et's review our journey so far.

We started at a roadblock, our own resistance to unfamiliar ideas, behaviors, and activities. After taking a moment to uncover ways to address that resistance, we surveyed the environment and named habits that got us to this point. Good and bad, antiquated or futuristic, these habits have come together to construct our path through society. We acknowledged that some habits need to be upgraded or repaired, and also recognized the virtue of fundamental habits such as curiosity, for they help prevent monotony and danger. We continued on by evaluating our own vehicle - our abilities. Doing so provided an opportunity to appreciate our faculties as well as our potential. Instead of being stuck on a familiar but overused road, we determined that we do in fact have the power to influence how we navigate the road ahead.

This final chapter discusses *availability* in terms of what we have and have access to to improve our path. This is critical because our work thus far has been meaningless if we have neither the time nor the tools to actually make changes.

Common sense - *the ability to make sound and prudent judgments based on simple perceptions of a situation or fact* - **is available to Americans**. For some, this means prioritizing fitness, health, companionship, and education. For others, it means prioritizing the steps we have taken in this book in order to better grasp reality.

Are you moving with life, against it, or not moving at all?
What tools <u>are</u> available to help you shape your life?

CHALLENGES TO AVAILABILITY

I don't usually wake up thinking *'I intend to do things I don't want to do today'*. It sounds ridiculous, but often we do just that. Working a boring job, commuting in heavy traffic, interacting with rude strangers, eating unsatisfying foods, wearing uncomfortable clothing, staying in unhealthy relationships, neglecting physical or mental health…the list goes on. It is profound to think of the number of activities we engage in (out of habit) that we actually don't want to do.

I could easily suggest that you quit your boring job or spend your next paycheck on new clothing, but there can be just as many *challenges to availability* as there are unwanted activities:

>*I don't have time to look for another job, much less go on multiple interviews.*

I lost/gained a lot of weight quickly due to an expensive medical emergency. I don't have money for a new wardrobe.

>*I work in Customer Service, rudeness is part of the job.*

My family can only afford to prioritize the quantity over the quality of groceries.

>*This is the fastest route to my job.*

We married young, so getting a divorce and becoming single at this age is scary.

>*I don't have health insurance / If I quit my job I won't have insurance.*

Navigating these challenges to availability is not always easy.

From January 2002 to September 2013, a replacement for the eastern span of the Bay Bridge was constructed in California. Bay Area residents were eager to experience the new sections' expanded lanes and modern architecture, but replacing a bridge that carries more than 250,000 vehicles a day[21] required a very important and equally inconvenient step - close the route completely in order to connect the new span.

As a Bay Area commuter during the second half of this construction, I can attest to the public's *resistance* to the project and its costs, *habitual* commutes that were **significantly** affected by closures and detours, and the workers' *ability* to complete the record-setting project safely. Project managers didn't let public pushback halt the project altogether. They held space for concerns to be discussed. Managers also used findings about commuter habits, environmental factors, and architectural and engineering limits to inform what they would be able to construct. Despite numerous setbacks, a new bridge was constructed by **finding, gathering, using, and accessing resources that were available**. It didn't happen magically or overnight, but through prudent and methodical behaviors.

In order to repair or replace our own path, it's imperative that we

HOLD SPACE FOR RESISTANCE

MAKE TIME FOR HABITS

AND

CREATE ENERGY FOR ABILITIES

41

HOLD SPACE FOR RESISTANCE

My mother just asked,
    "do people really tell you that they don't have time to meditate?"
Yes, they absolutely do.

In the same way that some Bay Area citizens preemptively declared that there was neither money nor time to replace the well-traveled bridge, many students have resisted wellness plans before their situation could even be assessed.

Common sense is not the same as using our instincts or preferences, aversions or fears to address problems. When those preferences or aversions show up in the form of resistance, it's important to create some room around them so that we don't make a situation worse.

Instead of making shortsighted statements,
we can wait to gather more information.

In lieu of becoming agitated during an argument,
we can withdraw from the situation and reassess what is happening.

Rather than letting discomfort trigger reactivity,
we can acknowledge discomfort and choose another activity to do.

Holding space for resistance makes it easier to see how significant a barrier really is. Wisely, my mother just responded that if someone told her they didn't have time to meditate, she would tell them to breathe. But before I lose you readers who think I'm about to recommend 'woo woo[22]' techniques, note that you can hold space for resistance by doing things that YOU actually want to.

42

WANTS, DESIRES, & GOALS

Look back at your reflection from the beginning of this chapter. Can you transform one or more of your wants into a *space-holder for resistance?*

Imagine you are in an uncomfortable disagreement with a coworker. Which of your *wants* could you do in the moment to hold space for the mounting tension? If wanting to meditate isn't on your list, for example, consider activities such as calling a friend or taking a walk.

By keeping track of the things that bring pleasure and purpose to our lives, we can visualize options for what to prioritize more easily.

Lists like this give our mind more positive points to focus on when situations make us uncomfortable. By giving that discomfort some space and redirecting our thoughts, we can eventually deal with the situation more rationally. What's more, goal-setting can also help to contain resistance. When uncomfortable situations make it hard to see the road we are on, a predetermined aim or intention can bring our attention back to the road.

In six months, for example, I want to have a different relationship with social media. Currently, when I feel resistance due to discomfort or boredom, I instinctively grab my phone and open a scrolling app. Scrolling through social media takes up more time than I like, so I want to reduce my usage of these apps. By simply remembering this goal AND reflecting on my list of wants, I can chose other ways to hold space for resistance (such as walking my dog, or making a cup of tea).

Identifying what we want - not just dwelling on our dislikes - is simple but takes practice. Fortunately, habits are available to help.

MAKE TIME FOR (GOOD) HABITS

A street sign can be replaced quickly, but it still takes time to print and cut. Potholes can be filled, but the filler still needs time to set. And bridges are simply not built in a day.

Many of the habits that define our lives have taken years (and in some cases generations) to establish, so it would be absurd to expect a radical overhaul overnight. In order to **make time for habits** we can use the space we created around resistance to tinker with established habits and try out new ones:

- *Introduce weekly flossing*
- *Join a friend who already takes fitness classes*
- *Plan and cook a dinner to test options for a diet you're considering*
- *Research and practice phrases that will help you excel socially/professionally*
- *Use one day a week to commute on a new route*
- *Pick a day in the month to initiate a tough or necessary conversation*
- *Pick a weekend to start learning a new skill*

Make time to lay the groundwork for the new habits you want as well as those that need calibrating. Carefully examine what works and what doesn't, what sources are useful or not credible. Poor-planning and hasty work can lead to disaster[23], but adequate preparation and composed performance can guarantee success.

ENCOURAGE THE ENERGY FOR ABILITIES

Children, family needs, illnesses, accidents, bills, lack of resources, jobs, hobbies, and many other factors are commonly used to excuse changes:

After a long day of work, taking care of my family, and doing laundry, I simply do not have any energy left for the things I want to do.

Furthermore, the bigger or more complex our desires are, the more daunting *challenges to availability* seem. This is why many projects, resolutions, and great ideas fail before they even begin.

Colleagues with monotonous 9 to 5 jobs have shared that the jobs are predictable and in some cases, do not encourage professional growth. Fellow entrepreneurs have shared that they've lost the enthusiasm that prompted them to start their own businesses due to the need to focus on profits or competition. Loved ones who are caretakers of their own children and other family members have also expressed feeling stuck. Either because they are literally reading at an elementary level daily for their child or because they remain hyper-focused on the needs of those dependent on their attention and care.

A common thread in these experiences is an energy deficit in the desired area. Instead of feeling recognized and supported to work hard on a project, for example, an employee feels unassisted under mounting pressure. The energy that could go into being excited about a project is redirected to being in survival-mode.

What we do frequently
...feeling stressed, sleeping inadequately, neglecting our own needs...
...feeling secure, resting, taking care of self...
determines our frequency (frequent-cy)

Encourage the energy needed for your abilities. If you want to become more flexible, spend more energy motivating yourself to do flexibility training than you spend complaining about it. If you want to achieve a financial or personal goal, use more effort to research and take steps forward than you use to regret how long it took you to start. If you don't want to be known as a negative person, fortify your inner 'bridge' of positivity and dismantle the fatigued road of negativity.

We each have 24 hours in a day.

Although we don't all have the same resources or energy levels, this statement is a nice reminder that we each have *something* to work with. *Encouraging energy* is another way to say <u>use what you've got</u>. Reserve small amounts of energy and then pour it into the moments you've made to slowly but surely enhance your abilities.

~ ~ ~

A NOTE ON LIVING AUTHENTICALLY

"Availability does not decrease your value. It tests the value of others."[24]
-Sandeep Suddarsi

Living authentically means *doing what we want* with our lives as well as making ourselves available to those things, people, places, and activities that are important to us. But doing what we want does not mean living impulsively. An authentic life uses available information (internal <u>and</u> external) to determine how we will respond to the world. And since Americans insist on *doing what we want*, it is vital that we examine the road we take to arrive at our own *authenticity*.

When the busy-ness of life becomes overwhelming and I feel like the world is out of control, I remember what someone once told me during an argument:

You have to participate in your life.

The words we use and clothes we wear, the speed we drive and texts we send (or 'leave on read'), are opportunities to live authentically. Take time to review the roles you play in your own life by using the tools available in this book to better understand how you show up in the world.

~~~

A BRIEF PLANNING GUIDE

The best plan is to plan well. Take your time to clearly name a goal, list the steps to reaching that goal, identify relevant challenges for each step, and take consistent actions in the direction of the goal. **HOWEVER**, when this type of thorough planning is not an option, we can resist the urge to simply give up. Instead, we can *figure it out* using skills we've acquired.

Break your want into smaller desires AND consider if your want is part of a much bigger desire.
> *When I become stressed, I don't want to _____ . I want to _____ .*
> *I also want to feel like I am _____ .*

Ask yourself what you are already doing to move towards the end goal.
> *I am already _____ . I also _____ regularly.*

Ask yourself what you are also *able* to do.
> *I am able to _____ , _____ , and _____ .*
> *If I have trouble with _____ , then I can _____ .*

Compare the things that you are able to do with those things you actually want to do.
> *Even though I am able to _____ , I don't really want to because _____ .*
> *An alternative to this is _____ because _____ .*

Consider what you can do to change those abilities into availabilities.
> *Doing _____ takes a lot of time and energy.*
> *Instead of _____ , I can _____ daily/weekly/monthly.*

Reflect on the role others can play in helping you reach the goal.
> *A list of people who can help me/keep me accountable are _____ .*
> *I trust them because _____ .*

CHAPTER 4 ASSIGNMENTS

WATCH/LISTEN TO AN EPISODE OF "THE PEOPLE I KNOW"
Season 4: The White Women I Know
www.joiofdance.org/thepeopleiknow

Use the link provided, pick an episode from the fourth season (or binge them all), and reflect on relevant concepts from this week's lesson.

FIND EXAMPLES OF AVAILABILITIES IN SOCIAL MEDIA

Set a timer for 5 minutes and see how many examples of AVAILABILITIES you can find online or in your social media feed.

The colloquial phrase *I have time* refers to one's availability to give attention to a subject…usually a dramatic event.
While scrolling this week, notice the subjects and activities people *have time for*. Consider whether, if you were in their positions, you would make yourself similarly available.

REFLECTION
Take 5-15 minutes to journal by hand, phone, audio or video.

1 - Reflect on things that are available to you - smart watches, budgeting apps, convenient travel, the internet… What resources are available to you to help you achieve the life you want?

2 - Reflect on the most difficult challenges to the available resources in #1. List possible solutions to these challenges even if they require something that are outside of your reach or resources.

CONCLUSION

The road to common sense doesn't start at complex political issues, egregious professional behaviors, or appalling national tragedies.

For the modern American, the road to common sense starts at our individual perspectives, well-established routines, comfort zones, assumptions and expectations. For a country that gives more attention and praise to individual achievement than it does to addressing collective needs, it only makes sense for this book to meet readers at their own driveway instead of on a shared freeway.

There is much more to discuss, and you should have more questions than answers, more concerns than solutions, right now.

A handful of the wealthiest and most influential humans on the planet gathered in America this week to celebrate new leadership - to figuratively create new signs for the road we use to travel as a society. Their signs don't alert us to imperfections in the road, address backlogs of construction requests, or acknowledge existing hazards. Instead, obstacles, threats, and dangers observed by non-experts[25] and experts[26] alike have been passed over and ignored.

It is unsettling that problems associated with poor reasoning seem to multiply by the day. It is disheartening to see that a country with global power & influence rankings of #1 simultaneously has a quality of life that ranks #22 - most notably due to safety, affordability, equality, and healthcare deficiencies[27].

But again, the road to common sense doesn't begin with national issues. National issues require strong critical thinking skills, and Americans are not ready to think critically.

~~~~~~~

Americans can get better at maneuvering individual differences.
American habits can be reexamined.
American's abilities (especially work-related ones) don't need exploitation.
Tools are available to help us reason prudently.

Resistance is natural.
Recognize it when it arises, hold space for it, and work to perceive your environment accurately.

Habits define our character.
Make time for good ones, recalibrate the bad ones, and remain curious about what you are doing.

Abilities can be improved.
Cultivate the energy you need to utilize your skills exceptionally.

Availabilities are all around us.
Elevate your perspective in order to address issues sufficiently.

-J-

AUTHOR BIOGRAPHY

Joi Cox is a multi-hyphenate based in Nevada, USA. She is a classically trained dancer, formally educated philosopher, and animal-loving wellness coach. Raised in a military family (Navy + Air Force) and reared primarily in the southern United States, her formative dance training led to 30+ years of performing arts that continues to this day.

After becoming intrigued by existential philosophers in secondary school, Joi proceeded to earn both Bachelor's and Master's degrees in the subject. She spent over five years formally teaching critical thinking, ethics, and introductory philosophy to community college students in-person and online.

Today, as a certified personal trainer and registered yoga teacher, Joi guides clients of all ages and ability levels to approach their wellness goals holistically.

WORKS CITED

[1] Burd-Sharps, Sarah, et al. "Road Rage Shootings Remain Alarmingly High." *Everytown Research & Policy*, 19 Dec. 2024, everytownresearch.org/road-rage-shootings-remain-alarmingly-high/.

[2] "Employee Misconduct on the Increase, Study Finds." *InterWest Insurance Services*, 2019, www.iwins.com/employee-misconduct-on-the-increase-study-finds/.

[3] Wallis, Jasmine. "What Is Breadcrumbing and How to Know If It's Happening to You." *VICE*, 23 May 2024, www.vice.com/en/article/what-is-breadcrumbing-how-to-know-if-its-happening-to-you/.

[4] Frishberg, Hannah. ""Roaching" Is the Newest Gross Trend to Infest the Dating World." *New York Post*, 27 Aug. 2021, nypost.com/2021/08/27/roaching-is-the-new-gross-trend-to-infest-the-dating-world/.

[5] Centers for Disease Control and Prevention. "Fast Facts: Health and Economic Costs of Chronic Conditions." *Chronic Disease*, 2024, www.cdc.gov/chronic-disease/data-research/facts-stats/index.html.

[6] Webster, Merriam. "Definition of COMMON SENSE." *Merriam-Webster.com*, 2019, www.merriam-webster.com/dictionary/common%20sense.

[7] Rietzschel, Eric F., Bernard A. Nijstad, and Wolfgang Stroebe, 'Why Great Ideas Are Often Overlooked: A Review and Theoretical Analysis of Research on Idea Evaluation and Selection', in Paul B. Paulus, and Bernard A. Nijstad (eds), *The Oxford Handbook of Group Creativity and Innovation*, Oxford Library of Psychology (2019; online edn, Oxford Academic, 9 May 2019), https://doi.org/10.1093/oxfordhb/9780190648077.013.11.

[8] Newman, Katelyn. "Obesity in America: A Public Health Crisis." *US News & World Report*, 19 Sept. 2019, www.usnews.com/news/healthiest-communities/articles/2019-09-19/obesity-in-america-a-guide-to-the-public-health-crisis.

[9] Gunja, Munira Z., et al. "U.S. Health Care from a Global Perspective, 2022: Accelerating Spending, Worsening Outcomes." *The Commonwealth Fund*, 2023, www.commonwealthfund.org/publications/issue-briefs/2023/jan/us-health-care-global-perspective-2022.

[10] Rainie, Lee, and Andrew Perrin. "Key Findings about Americans' Declining Trust in Government and Each Other." *Pew Research Center*, Pew Research Center, 22 July 2019, www.pewresearch.org/short-reads/2019/07/22/key-findings-about-americans-declining-trust-in-government-and-each-other/.

[11] Balch, Bridget. "We Can Solve Poverty in America. We Just Don't Want To." *AAMC*, 6 Nov. 2023, www.aamc.org/news/we-can-solve-poverty-america-we-just-don-t-want.

[12] Burd-Sharps, Sarah, et al. "Road Rage Shootings Remain Alarmingly High." *Everytown Research & Policy*, 19 Dec. 2024, everytownresearch.org/road-rage-shootings-remain-alarmingly-high/.

[13] Schmalbruch, Sarah, and Talia Lakritz. "What Fast Food Looks like in Real Life Compared to Photos." *Business Insider*, 31 Aug. 2018, www.businessinsider.com/fast-food-reality-versus-photos-promos-2017-3#in-this-photo-the-pizza-appears-pretty-greasy-12.

[14] Bounds, Dawn. "Social Media's Impact on Our Mental Health and Tips to Use It Safely." *UC Davis Health*, 10 May 2024, health.ucdavis.edu/blog/cultivating-health/social-medias-impact-our-mental-health-and-tips-to-use-it-safely/2024/05.

[15] Reddit Thread. "How Many Hours a Week Is Too Much for You." *Reddit.com*, 2024, www.reddit.com/r/work/comments/1bmv7tk/how_many_hours_a_week_is_too_much_for_you/.

[16] Bergland, Christopher. "Eight Habits That Improve Cognitive Function." *Psychology Today*, 2014, www.psychologytoday.com/us/blog/the-athletes-way/201403/eight-habits-that-improve-cognitive-function.

[17] Whitney, Constance. "How Chronic Negativity Can Affect Your Overall Health – Northern Iowa Therapy." *Nitherapy.com*, 2023, nitherapy.com/how-chronic-negativity-can-affect-your-overall-health/.

[18] "We Added 370 New Words to the Dictionary for September 2022." *Www.merriam-Webster.com*, Merriam-Webster, 2022, www.merriam-webster.com/wordplay/new-words-in-the-dictionary.

[19] Kasler, Karen. "Driven to Distraction: New Rules Recommend States Steer Clear of Highway Sign Humor." *NPR*, 19 Jan. 2024, www.npr.org/2024/01/19/1225370260/driven-to-distraction-new-rules-limit-those-humorous-state-highway-signs.

[20] Courtman, Tyrone. "Human Factors: The Dangers of "Confirmation Bias" | European Association of Turnaround Professionals." *Eactp.eu*, 2025, www.eactp.eu/news-and-events/article/human-factors-the-dangers-of-confirmation-bias.

[21] Wikipedia Contributors. "San Francisco-Oakland Bay Bridge." *Wikipedia*, Wikimedia Foundation, 15 Jan. 2019, en.wikipedia.org/wiki/San_Francisco–Oakland_Bay_Bridge.

[22] "Woo-Woo." *Merriam-Webster.com*, 24 Dec. 2024, www.merriam-webster.com/dictionary/woo-woo.

[23] Horgan, Rob. "FIU Bridge Collapse | Lessons Learnt Three Years since Florida Tragedy." *New Civil Engineer*, 15 Mar. 2021, www.newcivilengineer.com/latest/fiu-bridge-collapse-lessons-learnt-three-years-since-florida-tragedy-15-03-2021/.

[24] Nojoto. "Availability Does Not Decrease Your Value It Tests." *Nojoto.com*, 2023, nojoto.com/post/9514dec16f065c9984e44d0082bf7c7b/availability-does-not-decrease-your-value-it-tests-the-value-of-ot/.

[25] Loewentheil, Hannah. "Concerning Trends That Are Taking over Society Today." *BuzzFeed*, 8 Jan. 2025, www.buzzfeed.com/hannahloewentheil/concerning-modern-day-trends.

[26] "Surgeon General Urges Americans to "Rethink How We're Living Our Lives" in Closing Letter to the Country (Exclusive)." *People.com*, 2025, people.com/surgeon-general-vivek-murthy-americans-closing-letter-rethink-how-we-are-living-our-lives-exclusive-8770191.

[27] Ziegler, Brett. "United States Ranks among the World's Best Countries." *Usnews.com*, 2019, www.usnews.com/news/best-countries/united-states.

Made in the USA
Middletown, DE
10 February 2025